A Rebel's Heart

A
Rebel's
Heart

Remember Self

A Paved Visions Publication

Dedication

To my wife Vanessa,
for believing in me and pushing me to strive beyond reach.
Your unrelenting support helped turn a dream into a reality.
I love you forever.

To my parents,
for raising me to operate with an open mind and teaching
me to think outside the box. This journey wouldn't have
been possible without those life lessons.

Your King,
Remember Self

Copyright © 2023 Remember Self.

ISBN: 978-8-987-89481-1 (Paperback)
ISBN: 978-8-987-89480-4 (Ebook)

Any references to historical events, real people, or real places are used fictitiously. Names, characters, and places are products of the author's imagination.

Front cover image by Paved Visions
Book design by Paved Visions
Printed by IngramSpark, in the United States of America.

First printing edition 2023.

Paved Visions
New York

www.pavedvisions.com
info@pavedvisions.com

Contents

Underneath my Mask...9
Hourglass Feeling...10
The Blood of a Slave...11
Struggle and Tears...12
The Mental Warfare...13
Is it Worth the Pain...14
Concealed Intents...15
The One Who Got Away...16
Signs of Her Sorrow...17
Cinderella Dreams...18
Precious Thoughts...19
Opposites Attract...20
Erroneous Destiny...21
Mistaken Paradise...22
Two Broken Mirrors...23
Into the Eyes of God...24
Afraid to get Close...25
Struggle in my Eyes...26
My Eyes Tell a Story...27
Spiritual Warfare...28
To Fear a Loving God...29
No Such Thing as Sin...30
I'm Already a Legend...31
Secret of the Stars...32
Perfect Nightmare...33
Staring in a Mirror...34
Can I Have a Moment...35
A Tale of Two Cities...36
When Pain Runs Deep...37
No More Fire in Hell...38
Temptations of Man...39
He's a Two Time Felon...40
Dog Who Never Lived...41
Water Nine Planets...42
My Forbidden Fruit...43

Underneath My Mask

Unprepared for what lies ahead as I have no clue
No time for relaxing as I plan the next move
Distant I will seem, I'm just searching for my way
Even as I let you in, understood you could not say
Rescued by the devil, a blessing in disguise
Needed was the fire as he opened my eyes
Engulfed within the blaze, sparks began to kindle
Arose from the ashes he left on my window
The smoke began to clear, and the truth began to show
Hope then became alive, yet I still did not know
Mindful of the puzzle as I search for a piece
Yanked from my dream to find it already complete
Mirrors are now sharper, no more fog in the lens
Abstract is the goal, thus the patience starts to thin
Silence keeps you golden, thus there's no need to ask
Keep wondering to yourself what's underneath my mask

Hourglass Feeling

Hints are being ignored, though I notice they are here
Overlooked by these eyes that see nothing but fear
Unafraid of this page, but that to which it leads
Racing through the chapters, I start to sense the speed
Given a pick and an axe to dig my way out
Long road was taken, as if my wings couldn't sprout
All along there they were, sitting right on my back
Soared out into the sky and on to the next act
Serene pictures of art my eyes had failed to see
Formed with precision an engineer could not meet
Endless troves of beauty I was yearning to gain
Enticed the wrong desires, know that's part of the game
Lessons being taught, it's up to self to decode
I became informed so other minds I must mold
Nervous I became as I headed towards the ceiling
God smirked and said, it's just an hourglass feeling

The Blood of a Slave

Tears continue to fall for the blind fail to see
How the wounds we thought were healed continue to leak
Even as the sun sets, she gives hints clear as day
Blowing with the wind are the answers in your face
Let your mind paint the canvas, these words are your brush
Only ask you take your time, no need for the rush
Open your pretty eyes and paint the picture you see
Diamonds in the sky, or is it blood on the leaves
Or maybe it's a sun with a smile that shines bright
Flowers it could be that shed tears throughout the night
Among them are the clouds who know not what to say
Since it's they who are confused, thus white turns into gray
Listen to the pictures that you have just painted
Allow them to embed without worries of being tainted
Vindication in my heart, I'll take to the grave
Every picture I paint shows the blood of a slave

Struggle and Tears

Sheaths start to erode as the soul becomes weak
Tears fail to cease as the future becomes bleak
Roads seem to vanish, so you're forced to change the route
Unseen was the curve, here comes the cloud they call doubt
Gloom nestles in the heart as you search for a path
Gears hesitate to shift thus you run out of gas
Looking in the rearview not knowing what's ahead
Engraved in your mind is every tear that was shed
As you continue to chase the shadows of bliss
Note how they're elusive, you always seem to miss
Dreams you had as a child seem to go down the drain
Though the odds are low, a ray of hope still remains
Escape you wish you could but there's nowhere to turn
Ashamed of how the masses sit and watch you burn
Refugee in your home for the past twenty years
Started with joy, now it's all struggle and tears

The Mental Warfare

Through altered perceptions, all tactics will remain
Hidden in plain sight along with rules to the game
Ensnared within a web wove with lies and deceit
Mistiness of the eyes results in failure to peep
Elusive by design but still not hard to find
Notice the illusions, observe them blow your mind
The wise move in silence, yet find a way to teach
As they walk through the maze others deem incomplete
Liberation is at hand, but one must first know
Where the hidden chains reside, or one cannot grow
Awkward thoughts will arise for the path is unknown
Removal of the veil shows the path was not wrong
Forbidden fruit was given to make one believe
Apples must have fallen from orange bearing trees
Renovating the web as the truth becomes bare
Enslaved within this game called the mental warfare

Is it Worth the Pain

Intentions were always pure, but my windshields were cracked
So my vision was shattered and inspiration I lacked
Ignorant of the tears that fell behind the smile
Thinking one day soon we'll be walking down that aisle
Wary you became of my deceitful actions
Only thing you did was deepen your passion
Ready I was not though I wish I would have been
The sun would still be shining had I learned to be a man
Hope your heart has mended and your scars have healed
Though I have accepted that mine never will
Hard as I have tried, I just can't seem to move on
Even though I wish I could, your heart was my home
Pretended not to hurt whenever you crossed my mind
Acted as if I didn't care, though I knew I was lying
Images still arise and they still hurt the same
Never will I question, is it worth the pain

Concealed Intents

Captured by the web that was carefully spun
Open eyes couldn't see that the battle was won
Numbered are your days for you could not see
Careful observations as you paced the lonely streets
Enticed by desires from behind closed doors
Although it was shown, and the option was yours
Little did you know, it was the one you didn't expect
Even though it appeared he was here to protect
Demons begun to glimpse, but the truth was ignored
Intimate thoughts are invaded like never before
Notice the illusions thrown into the vision
Taken for granted thus reality is missing
Evidence becomes stronger, eyes become weaker
Nights become darker, no sign of the teacher
Trust no more, for nothing makes sense
Since you failed to see the concealed intents

The One Who Got Away

Two became one, then one became two again
Hope left the scene, disrupting the entire plan
Eventually the stars disappeared from the sky
Opaque the clouds became as they prepared to cry
Never did this scenario cross my mind
Ending something so special and hard to find
Whenever I reflect, my heart always smiles
Hearing your voice daily, though it's been a while
Open heart and open arms, you know I'm always yours
Gates will never close, you have the keys to the door
Once it was too late, I realized who you were
True angel from above with a heart that's so pure
A blessing in disguise, the definition of love
Warrior by nature but sweet as a dove
A ray of light with every breath that you take
You know who you are, the one who got away

Signs of her Sorrow

Since that rainy day, the sun never rose again
Incomplete I became, never was I whole again
Getting stronger is the pain that rests in my heart
Nothing is the same, I wish that I could restart
Staring in the rearview, I see my selfish ways
Opened hells gates with a smirk on my face
Fire didn't burn me until it was too late
Here I am now looking at an empty place
Each day that passes, I hurt a little more
Realizing her pain that I never saw before
Something in her eyes told me to be aware
Overlooked them with ease as if I didn't care
Red they became as the anger grew inside
Rope was then cut but I couldn't see it with my eyes
Only if I had known there would be no tomorrow
Would have paid attention to the signs of her sorrow

Cinderella Dreams

Covert feelings finally begin to surface
Instant were the smiles, open were the curtains
Next was a name to match a beautiful face
Desperate I became as I yearned for a place
Entertaining thoughts were constant on my mind
Respected your position as I waited on my time
Entwined with a feeling I 've never felt before
Love I know it was, though I failed to show you more
Lost sight of our vision somewhere down the road
Acted like I didn't care, as if my heart was so cold
Damage was done but it was my goal to repair
Rectify the pain and show you that I care
Expect no more pain nor broken promises
All these lonely years, your smile I dearly miss
Making a promise to always be on your team
Soon I shall fulfill all your Cinderella dreams

Precious Thoughts

Picture perfect, something we could never be
Racing time, chasing something we could never see
Embrace who you are, accept all of your flaws
Can't you see we all have them, both big and small
Imagine life with no evil and all was good
One without the other, we'd be misunderstood
Unbalanced, the world would be nothing but chaos
Starting with the atom, the very thing that make us
Take the time to see all of life has symmetry
Head of the cosmos to the bottom of the sea
Once this is understood life will make more sense
Ultimate goal of life is to get across the fence
Go ahead and look around, the answers are there
Help is in your face, but you remain unaware
The key is in your hand, the battle has been fought
Sharing with you one of my most precious thoughts

Opposites Attract

Orange skies hovered as the moon began to peak
Personal opinions made the future look weak
Problems arose because we didn't understand
Or open our lonely eyes to see the bigger plan
Some ways we're so different, although we're the same
I give you all the credit, and I'll take the blame
Together we'll be until the end of time
Even though we're far apart, you're constant on my mind
Something in my heart tells me I'm not alone
Although I can't confirm, I know I'm not wrong
Though you're an angel and I'm more of the demon
The bond we had was perfect, I know you can see it
Ready to pick up the pieces of a shattered dream
Accept the feeling in your heart, let's start clean
Can you forever fight the truth? Look deeply at that
Since you see it for yourself, that opposites attract

Erroneous Destiny

Even though it feels wrong, you find room to believe
Running in the dark, thinking you could achieve
Racing down the aisle due to what you were told
Only if you took the time to light up the road
Now that you've gotten the hint, open your eyes
Expect to be surprised by the centuries of lies
One's fate is sealed, for that book has been published
Understand you cannot fail, live your life, and love it
Some performed miracles, know that you could do the same
Dancing with doubt shall keep you on the right train
Escape the chains of faith, until you truly know
Shed the skin of lies and watch the source grow
Take all the time you need, though it doesn't exist
In the light you'll see why the masses resist
Now you know the secret, you say you'll use the key
Yet you still chase your erroneous destiny

Mistaken Paradise

Miniature seeds can sprout the biggest of trees
If you know your potential and simply believed
Serenaded by the words you deemed to be true
Took them for granted, they did the thinking for you
All you can envision, is the heaven in the sky
Kingdoms filled with mansions and angels by your side
Eden is the goal, so you strive to be a saint
Never will you make it standing on an empty tank
Problem starts within, for you failed to deeply delve
Accepted the lies without a look for yourself
Remember who you are, it has been said many times
Age after age but you have chosen to be blind
Distractions everywhere to keep your mind occupied
Intricately designed and it's working overtime
Sure enough you know deep down what is right
Even as you search for a mistaken paradise

Two Broken Mirrors

Tainted visions lead to answers without questions
Water fills the lungs, but you see it as a blessing
Once you figure out that you are slowly drowning
Beautiful smiles will become tearful frowning
Rake up all the leaves and you'll remember the grass
Open all the windows and stop looking through glass
Kings and Queens you wish to be, but you fail to see
Echelon is backwards because you missed the scheme
Naked and afraid in the middle of a storm
Many cast the bait, only few have bitten the worm
If you do not go within, you'll only go without
Resting in the depths of a lonely dark cloud
Rearrange your thoughts to find a better way
Omit the money, know there is a better pay
Reaching for stars won't make it any clearer
Since you fail to notice the two broken mirrors

Into the Eyes of God

Is it real or is it fake, will it ever be too late
Napping so long, it feels strange to be awake
Time is of an essence, yet it is an illusion
Opening the doors to satisfaction and confusion
Take a peek behind the curtain, tell me what you see
Hope for the future or a past that was bleak
Entertain the thought, your mind shall surely ponder
Everything you were taught from above and down under
Yet you still question though the truth began to show
Every single option paved out the same road
Stars will realign when the sun begins to shine
Open your darkened eyes, let the light into your mind
Feel the power of freedom as you travel back home
Gaining everything you lost from that sweet & sad song
On your way to redemption, the peas are out the pod
Delighted as you stare into the eyes of God

Afraid to get Close

Angels in the sky, horns poking from their head
Fire in the eyes, spoke the words they never said
Ring of death is near, but somehow you escape
Acting like its luck but knowing it was fate
Insecure thoughts lead to a puzzled mind
Distant is the past once the future you find
Tangled in web that you've woven yourself
Only then will you see it's only you that can help
God is the answer, know that God is in You
Echoes that you hear, know that's God speaking truth
Treasure what you have, but I only ask why
Closed the eyes remain as the devil starts to cry
Left for you to enter but you drown yourself in fear
Open doors remain, wishing you would come here
Stairs erase as you climb, yet you still make the most
Even though you're afraid, afraid to get close

Struggle in my Eyes

See it all in my face yet you act surprised
Trouble everywhere I turn, eyes will tell no lies
Reach for the stars is what my teachers told
Unaware that the stars were only down the road
God made the plan, but God is really man
Get the picture now, understand what I am saying
Learn to live life and let go of all your fears
Everything was meant to happen, you'll learn through the years
Is it too much, if so, then wipe your eyes
Navigate within and see what lies inside
Make your way through the maze, note everything you see
Yell all you want but only you can hear the scream
Each day you get closer to no more nights itself
Yet you fail to reach for books upon the shelf
Even though you know that I have become wise
Still, you do not see the struggle in my eyes

My Eyes Tell a Story

Mirror hanging on my wall tells me all I need to know
Yearning for answers but my wings fail to glow
Excitement shows in one, but fear is in the other
Yet I fail to see they are related like a brother
Even though my pupils show the answers I need
Something isn't right, my mind is still not free
Trouble in paradise, or is it trouble at all
Even as the question is answered, I continue to fall
Live and let live, let nature take her course
Life is a game, there's no need to send a morse
Always be assured, never doubt your position
Sit back and relax, open your ears, and just listen
Tell me what you heard; did it scare you away?
Or did you take heed to a game you chose to play
Recognize it or not, there's no need to ever worry
Yet you can't see that my eyes tell a story

Spiritual Warfare

Started scratching that itch, tried to figure it out
Picture looking fuzzy, but it's starting to sprout
Itch turned into a fire, so I dug a little deeper
Realized all along, I was Him and the Reaper
Instantly both sides started tugging away
Taking turn after turn, so I ate off both plates
Under no condition shall I slide and retreat
Abyss is too deep, nowhere to land your feet
Let it all soak, watch it sit and dissolve
While the movie's still playing, though the TV is off
Anger turns into fear, for it was all a game
Reaching for stars that were meant to bring pain
Follow your heart, no longer lie to yourself
Allow them to guide, but only you take the step
Reflections of my mirror told me to be aware
Exposed me to the truth of this spiritual warfare

To Fear a Loving God

To fear a loving God is the biggest lie we were told
Open your eyes and see you have a much larger role
Few know the truth although it's available to all
Elevate your awareness to get over that wall
Advantage is in your hands, you only must listen
Remembering you is key, now pay close attention
All of us were here before and may be back again
Love is all we are so it's impossible to sin
Occupying the flesh to experience and recreate
Viewing ourselves separate from God is our biggest mistake
If we realize this, all else will follow suit
Now understand, we are the branches, He is the root
God gave us Free Will without any restrictions
Good can't be known without evil; see what you've been missing?
Opinions may vary and most will find it odd
Disbelief is expected, but you can't fear a loving God

No Such Thing as Sin

No such thing as sin, this you should know
One-tracked minds allow this theory to grow
Sent to this world to Re-Member and create
Under no circumstance are we punished for our mistakes
Children of God, we can do no wrong
Higher Evolved Beings was the plan all along
There is no distinction between wrong and right
He only observes and guides us toward the light
Indeed, this sounds bizarre, yet it is true
Navigate within yourself and you'll find the truth
Greatness awaits those who find they are the way
Always know whatever happens is what we create
Separated we can never accomplish our task
Since we all are one, we are first as well as last
Insane as it may sound, this is how it goes
No such thing as sin, this you now know

I'm Already a Legend

Inside is a voice informing you to closely listen
Make sure to hear these words, pay close attention
Always knew I was destined to make history
Late to the party but I still solved the mystery
Rough roads only helped strengthen my tires
Eating food for thought became my only desire
Acting all along as if nothing was on my mind
Dreaming I was, knowing it was almost my time
You could never understand if I stay too far ahead
Asking for explanations for the words that were said
Let it rest on your pinnacle, the answers will come
Even the feeblest of minds deserve to see the sun
Gears are now shifting, it's your onus to keep pace
End is slowly approaching, but there is no such place
No brakes to slow me down, life will always be pleasant
Don't fail to hear the message, I'm already a legend

Secret of the Stars

Staring at the sky into the darkness of the night
Emitting a light so bright though it's far out of sight
Creative alignments in every direction they behold
Reaching for the questions to the answers they showed
Embrace the signs that are constantly provided
Time will come when you can no longer hide it
Oh the power that they hold, yet we do not see
For even they shape our traits and personalities
Think of your likes and all the hobbies you love
Help was given to you from the guides above
Enhance your awareness, the road will appear
Soon you shall realize that it was always near
Take your time as failure is not a potential
All you need is to evaluate your credentials
Reasons will be known, healed will be the scar
Solved will be the riddle to the secret of the stars

Perfect Nightmare

Picture images that remind you of a desolate hour
Emitting sinister thoughts due to waning of power
Remember the pain that stung you in your heart
For you assumed your perfect life was falling apart
Each day that passed removed a little more faith
Creating desperate and distraught looks on your face
Trouble was constantly trailing, causing much sorrow
Nights became a time of wishing for no tomorrow
In the process of coping, did a light start to beam
Giving you a theory of the reasons for this scene
Hope started to reappear, and faith became clear
Triumph is now closer, finish line is finally near
Maybe it wasn't as bad as it appeared to be
All you needed to change was the way you perceive
Remember the images of that hour if you dare
Eventually you'll believe in the perfect nightmare

Staring in a Mirror

Single mind filled with many heartless thoughts
Thinking of the dreams and visions he once sought
Acting like he's happy, but deep down he feels pain
Reaching for answers as he's drowning in the rain
Inside he's lost, you can see it through his eyes
Nobody to turn to, no one will hear his lies
Graveyards waiting on him to sever his line
Instead, he escapes the reapers wicked mind
Now is the time or his day will never arrive
Allowing him to catch all others by surprise
Made a promise to get it together and move on
It was his intention, but the devil tagged along
Ready or not the demons are here to stay
Rooks got him in check, now he's ready to play
Opened his eyes, he felt the heat getting nearer
Realizing all along he was staring in a mirror

Can I Have a Moment

Can I have a moment to loosen the chains
Alleviate the tears and erase all the pain
Now is the key for it is all that exists
Images are real, so be careful as you wish
Hell that you envision, is nothing more than that
Another dirty tactic to keep one on his back
Vital to know, you visit home every night
Empty tanks are then filled to continue your flight
Astronomical trips once you catch the right wave
Must refrain from evil thoughts that sleep during the day
Operation is so simple, but yet it's so complex
Magic to the mind that miss the end of this text
Enduring to the end should be the least of worries
Now is what's important, I repeat with a flurry
Truth will never change, only lies and deception
Guess the moral of the story, is learn to use your blessing

A Tale of Two Cities

As the breath manifests all that you see
The wicked wonder if they could truly be
Another angel standing next to you and me
Little do they know, they are already complete
Evil lies within even the purest of souls
Only they control what the rest of us show
Feeling was always there, but the hill becomes steep
Therefore the comfort sets in and no longer they seek
Wisdom is the road that leads to understanding
Once you have the knowledge, you'll know who really planned it
Caught on the fence as you try to figure it out
Intense is the urge to continue heading south
Travel as you wish but North is always home
In time you'll make it, there's no rush, you're not alone
Entertainment is the key, enjoy it while you're with me
Science of these words is a tale of two cities

When Pain Runs Deep

What if all else fails and you have nothing to lose
Hate replaces love and scars grow from a bruise
Egos take a turn down a road that's well paved
Next comes a feeling not even Jesus could save
Private thoughts begin flirting with the devil
Asking him questions as he hands you the shovel
Inquiring even more as you fail to feel complete
Not knowing if the answers are really what you need
Rain is getting heavy, but the fire seems to grow
Understanding less the more the answers seem to show
Naked and afraid though the mirror shows you clothed
Scenes from this movie are being cut and untold
Dance will continue, this is the route that was chosen
Even the devil has times Hell seems to be frozen
Evening has arrived, the tears start to seep
Problems of the soul, when pain runs deep

No More Fire in Hell

Nevermind what you were told, look for yourself
Of another dusty classic sitting deep on the shelf
Memorize what you forgot if you could handle the task
Or simply let it be and you can drop out of class
Routes do not matter; destinations are the same
End up where you wish, still nothing more than grain
Fishing for a bigger picture, something you can't see
It can only be felt when you locate the key
Releasing the chains that were bound at your feet
Even though it's the mind that you really set free
Innocent they may seem, look deeper in their eyes
Note everything you see, watch how they act surprised
Hoping you would look past their devilish ways
Entertain them though they know they're losing their place
Long live the truth, she shall always prevail
Looking down and I see no more fire in hell

Temptations of Man

Touching her soul as she leads you away
Excitements at a high because she gave you a taste
Mirror is so broken but what you see is so clear
Posing for the camera while ignoring your fear
Thou shall not sin, but the demons are strong
As they whisper in your ear, and they sing you a song
Telling you stories that you know will break your home
Instead of your gut, you follow lies that break your own
Opened the door, now the guests refuse to leave
Nod their heads and smile as you continue to sleep
Sitting in the dark wondering how did you stray
Out of something so solid, how did you blemish your faith
Fire starts to get bigger, so the heat gets worse
Mind continues racing while you search for the curse
As the world turns, your face is deep in your hands
Never underestimate the temptations of man

He's a Two Time Felon

His hope has diminished, and his options are few
Even though he knows exactly what he's to do
Sit back and watch as the story unfolds
Ache was in his heart from the lies he was told
Truth was in the pudding, but the lies were so deep
Woven as a child so you know it's concrete
Only if his parents knew, the pain wouldn't seep
To the depths of a soul full of clouds and deceit
Inside are the cries for the tears can't be shown
Mind is so gone that he feels all alone
Eating every bullet, as if he's not even phased
Feeling every wound, though you never see the daze
Even in the fire, he seems to stay cool
Leading you on, to believe what you choose
Only if you knew he was deep into seven
Never would have guessed he's a two-time felon

Dog Who Never Lived

Danger in the heavens below, peace in the hells above
Objectifying dreams that were created from the drugs
Grown as a child although childish as an adult
Windows darken during the day as you follow the cult
Happy beginnings often lead to sad endings
Once the grave is dug, the soul starts his winning
Never for the weak because the weak lost the race
Etch it down a notch so all could get a taste
Veered down a dark road to be left all alone
Even as the masses tell you the path leads to home
Rigged minds and porcupines result in endless unrest
Level down another notch for ones who can't catch
Indecisiveness results in irrational decisions
Victory was mapped out with engineered precisions
Eager are the depths but on the surface are the fears
Diary this is, of the dog who never lived

Water Nine Planets

Watered plants that refuse to grow
Are results of roots that refuse to know
The value of the liquid that's needed to show
Every vine in an orchid that's needed to blow
Rather be alone until the age starts to flow
Near dreadful numbers where grays begin to glow
Insisted on being the only star of the show
Not knowing eight others required the same road
Eight outside of you, therefore you are the one
Playing the game as it's written, though the chapter is done
Leading the way is the brightest of them all
Allowing one to nourish without telling Him the fall
Never was it rough it just needed to be sanded
Even as it smooths, you may seem to be stranded
Truth shall prevail even as the others planned it
Sun Himself, still has to water nine planets

My Forbidden Fruit

Maybe it's too much, maybe it's just enough
You'll never know until you examine her touch
Freezing rain in the summer will keep you down under
Overly brazen storms shining bright as they stun her
Rainbows feel alone, showing a singular hue
Bathing butt naked in a waterless pool
Indeed, yes she knows, how unfaithful the seed
Dire is the need, that's the way that it seems
Drenched with an umbrella and conspicuous views
Eyes turn red as you're left with the blues
Nose towards the wind and still didn't catch a scent
Fire down below as you tried to present
Ruse that was played, you were just a recruit
Understood the message but still carried a suit
In case she changed her mind and fiddled the flute
Trekking down a lonely road, with my forbidden fruit

"Never dim your light at the expense of another. Shine it so bright that anyone around can't help but to see their own"

-Remember Self

PAVED VISIONS